MW01492008

How To Sell Used And New Items On eBay And Amazon: Insider Secrets Top Online Sellers Don't Want You To Know

Rick Grubb

FORWARD

This book is a book bundle of my two top selling eBooks **How to Start an Online Bookstore,** and **How to sell on eBay**. Together you will learn the basics of selling on eBay and Amazon, and will be able to successfully get a real online business up and running starting as soon as today.

HOW TO SELL ON EBAY: A SIMPLE START TO EBAY CONTENTS

Rick Grubb

INTRODUCTION

So many books about eBay are so complex and difficult to understand. When I started out selling on eBay there were no guides, and nobody to show me anything. I had to learn everything myself. This book will be a simple step by step guide to show you what I have learned over the years. You will learn how to find an item to sell all the way to collecting the money.

To start selling on eBay can be intimidating at first but once you learn how you will be an eBay pro. I will teach you a few tricks for making your listing look better and ways to write your descriptions to sell your items for more money.

EBay is a fortune 500 company, and one of the most

visited websites on the internet. Millions of people are on eBay every day buying and selling everything you can imagine. I have personally used eBay to make me thousands of dollars over the years and would like to teach you my step by step system to finding and selling items on eBay...

I will teach you

- how to choose winning items to sell

- how to find them, how to list them

- what to charge for them

- how to ship them

- what to do after the sale

- how to collect your money

- file taxes

- Even some nice advanced techniques.

I have been an eBay seller since 2000 and have been doing it ever since. I know my way in and out of eBay better than most and will prove it to you by the end of this book.

WHY SELL ON EBAY

EBay is easy to use, known around the world, and has great support and staff. The global marketplace that eBay has produced is something we may never see out of a company again. You can sell goods in dozens of countries all over the world.

GETTING STARTED ON EBAY

EBay is a very simple platform to buy and sell on. I will walk you through, step by step, exactly how I list my items for sale. Image finding an item, listing it on eBay, and a few days later having some extra money in your bank account.

Where to start

First you need to sign up for two accounts if you do not already have them. They are an eBay account and a PayPal account. PayPal is a payment processing company owned by eBay. They will handle collecting the money from your buyer for you. It is not necessary to have a PayPal account to sell on eBay but it pretty much is the only way people pay for items there.

Create an eBay account

Creating an account is easy on eBay. Just got eBay.com and click register on the top left of the screen and follow the simple instructions to get setup.

Create a PayPal account

Signing up for PayPal is also simple and since they are owned by eBay they will link your accounts together and make the sales process as simple as possible for you and your buyers. Simply got Paypal.com and on the main screen click "sign up for free." You will need your bank account information handy and PayPal will do a few test transactions into your account to confirm that you are the account holder.

Different ways to sell on eBay

There are different ways to sell on eBay. I personally say you should learn the system by selling your own stuff then move into different selling approaches. Let's talk about the different approaches though so you may have knowledge of them.

Consignment

Consignment means selling someone else's stuff for money. This is a good model but with a few flaws. You only get a percentage of the sale usually 25%-50%. That's all fine and dandy if the item sells for $100 but what if it only sells for $5 then you put a lot of work into a listing for nothing. To insure you make money regardless if the item sells or not you can charge a listing fee deposit. If the item does not sell you keep the money for your time. If it does then you can take the percentage and give them back there deposited. I have done this way before and it does work well. Plus all the items are brought to you so you do not have to go out looking for things to sell.

There is a place on eBay that you can list your consignment services which you can find here (add link) or go to (add link). This model is a great place to start a business but make sure you know what you are doing first. Get your feet wet with your own items. Then if you want to sell someone's stuff starts with family or friends first. Work your way up to strangers.

EBay store

An eBay store is a great way to expand your business. An eBay store will run about $15 a month and up. The nice thing about an eBay store is that once your customer has made it into your store you are not competing with everyone else on eBay.

Items listed in an eBay store are all going to be fixed price. This could be good or bad. The best way to promote your eBay store is to include a link on your auction page as well as on your invoice slips. More on this later.

EBay power seller status

The power seller status means you made a certain amount of money or sales in a given month. This gets you cheaper listing fees, as well as a stamp of approval from eBay. People will buy from you more often that those who are not power sellers because you are a more authority figure.

Fees

There are listing fees and final value fees you will have to pay. You will also have to pay a PayPal fee. For a complete list of eBay fees please click here. Or go to http://pages.ebay.com/help/sell/insertion-fee.html#fvf.

Rules

EBay is a simple site to sell on but you must play by the rules. For a complete list of all the rules and regulations please visit eBay's rules and policies page or go to http://pages.ebay.com/help/policies/overview.html .

FINDING AND LISTING YOUR FIRST ITEMS

Selling your own stuff

Start out on eBay by selling you own items you do not want anymore. Pretend you are going to have a garage sale. What in your house would you sell at your garage sale? Some of those old books? How about those old shoes, maybe even clean out your attic. Find about 10 items you are willing to sell. Practice listing your items and writing descriptions about them.

Once you have those items move on to the next step.

Getting your feet wet

We are going to use those items you found to get
your feet wet and learn the ropes of eBay. It really
does not matter if these sell for much or not. I want
to teach you the process that goes into listing an
item and the post processing of shipping and
collecting the money for these items. I should
mention that all of these items will probably not
sell. Although they might please do not get
discouraged and give up. Sometimes you may need
to relist an item three or four times before it sells.

How to List Items

The easiest way to list an item on eBay is to do a
search on eBay for the items you want to list. Once
you find that item, click on the listing and this will
take you to the listing page. From the listing page
scroll down a bit and look right below the main
image. There will be a button that says "Have One
to Sell" "Sell It Yourself". Click this link which will
then take you to the "create a listing page".

When you click that sell it yourself button it fills in
the title, generic description if there is one and the
categories. This is a huge help because those are
items and categories someone already took the

time to locate and figure out. From here will fill in the description, get a template, add pictures, and enter our shipping details.

Getting a Template

The first thing you need to do to make your listing stand out is to get a template. Templates will add a nice colorful background and will enhance your listing to make it stand out from the rest of the crowd. A template is one easy and quick way to potentially get more money for the same item everyone else is selling. I have been using templates for years and have proven that you can get more money and more bids just by adding a template.

Use.com

I love the site use.com. I cannot remember why or how I stumbled on this site but it really is a great site for eBay listing templates and even better than that they will host multiple photos for you. This is great news because eBay will charge a fee for adding extra photos through eBay on your listing. You can however have unlimited photos hosted on external websites such as use.com.

How to Choose a Template from Use.com

From the home screen on use.com go to templates tab. You will need to choose a template that fits with your item. When I sold a bunch of model airplane accessories a while back, I choose a background with the image of a plane on it. If you are selling some kind of baseball memorabilia then add a baseball theme to your listing.

There are hundreds of templates to choose from just start browsing around. Try to make your listing look really nice by choosing an appropriate template to go with it. Once you find a background, use.com give you some choices on how you want the page to display; (example: photos on the top, photos in the middle, or photos on the bottom of the text.)

I feel that the photo is the most important part of your listing so the photo should always go first or on top, followed by the thumbnail photos, and finally the text.

Next you will need to write in your item description, upload your photos, and get the html code for your template.

Click to watch my video on creating an ebay template wit Use.com or go to http://rickgrubb.com/video-training-on-creating-an-ebay-template-with-use-com/

Writing a description that sells

When writing a description for eBay you want to be as descriptive as possible. Do not leave anything out. For example, if I listed a simple desk lamp I would include the color, style, wattage, what type of light bulbs it uses, if there are any scratches, is it new or used, etc.

I also suggest you tell a story with your listing. Stories sell and stories paint a picture in people's minds. Give the story of the item, where you bought it, why it is so important, etc. Also use selling words like imagine, finally, perfect, inviting, cozy, you'll fall in love with, or any other type of phrases you can come up with. A great book for that is called words that sell. I own a copy of it and suggest anyone serious about eBay to do the same. You will be able to make your listings pop and sell better with the addition of just a few simple words.

List benefits not the features

Over the years of selling and marketing online I have learned people don't care about the features of a product, they care about the benefits and how it will help them.

If I were to sell cake decorating kits I would say something like "wow your friends with this amazing cake decorating kit. Using a simple border tip and a speed icier tip you can have a professional looking cake made right out of your own home". If you noticed I told them what they are getting. They are getting a border tip and a speed ice tip, and that you will be able to decorate professional looking cakes with this kit. I told them what they are getting and what it can do for them which is decorate professional looking cakes and wow their friends.

Price

What should I start my auction price at? This is a question I hear all the time. First of all we want our first items to be auction style listings. Right now eBay gives you the first 50 listing you create every month free then after that the fees to list an item are as followed.

$0.01-$0.99 = $0.10

$1-$9.99 - $0.25

$10-$24.99 = $0.50

$50-$199.99 = $1

$200+ = $2

These fees apply even if your item does not sell. This is how eBay makes their money. Just follow my listing strategies and you will soon be able to sell almost all of your listing and get exactly the amount of money your item is worth.

What I want you to do in the beginning while you are learning are to start your listings with a price of $0.99. Why? In my experience starting the auction out at $0.99 will make your item more flattering to people and draw attention to them to place a bid.

In the history of eBay an item with bids on it becomes more popular and draws people's attention better than an item with no bids. This is a huge benefit to you because once someone places a bid they feel like they own the item and will get into bidding wars with other people over it. In their mind they already own the item so once a person comes in to try to take it away they will bid more. This is one of the best kept secrets on eBay and the sellers who know it are raking in the money.

If you list an item and you know you need to make a certain amount then start the auction out at that price. Say my lamp I know I need to get $10 then I would start my auction out at $9.99.

By the way another good rule of listing, always have your price end in .99. This number will always sell better that a whole number such as 1.

Buy it now

Buy it now is another feature of eBay you see a lot of sellers. Buy It Now allows buyers to purchase an item before the first bid. You may start a buy it now at 20% higher than the starting bid. This is good to set at the amount you want to get for your item. Example: If I was selling that lamp I would start the auction at $0.99, however I could set the buy it now too $9.99 if that is the price I was hoping to get from the auction. This way you get impulse buyers or someone who might need that item now to purchase and you still get your asking price.

EBay includes 50 free buy it now offers with your 50 free auctions but I would wait to use these until you get used to listing an auction and go through the steps that you need to collect your money, ship a package, etc. Once you feel more comfortable and you learned how to check what other products of the same type are selling, which you will learn later, then you can go from there and start using buy it now features in your listings.

Shipping

When listing an item you must choose between shipping varies by location or fixed price shipping. I personally almost always use the shipping varies based on customer location. This is how I do it but it may not be the best way of doing it. If you have flat rate priority boxes, which I will go over shortly, then you can choose to ship on fixed price shipping.

Always pack your item before you list them too. This way all you have to do is weigh it with a small postage scale which you can buy on eBay and you are good to go.

Free shipping boxes

The post office has free shipping boxes available for flat rate priority and regular priority shipping. If you do not have a scale or do not wish to weigh your items I would suggest you use a flat rate priority shipping box. The prices range from $5.00 to $10.90 for most flat rate boxes. Check out more information at Ebay shipping supplies or go to http://ebaysupplies.usps.com/usps.

International shipping

International shipping is a much more complex ballgame. International shipping is expensive especially priority mail. If you plan to offer international shipping, which you should, I recommend having some boxes lying around that are not priority boxes so you can give your international customers a cheaper shipping option. For international shipping I always include parcel post, or first class shipping which will require non-priority shipping boxes from you. These shipping options are much cheaper for international shipping.

Images

Images are important to help sell an item. EBay gives you one free image but like I discussed earlier if you go to use.com you can add up to ten more photos and have them host the images instead of eBay. Let me explain this a bit further. If you click on an image within the eBay listing that is hosted by use.com it will open a new window at use.com and show you the pictures there. This is a great and easy way to save some money and list a bunch of pictures for your product. Pictures sell the product. Without a picture your item will either not sell or will not sell for the price it should.

How many images

A lot of people ask me how many images should be on a listing. I always say, five images should be the minimum you should have on your listing. There are exceptions such as a boxed item. Then an image of the front and rear of the box will do. Try to get close ups, different angles, etc. Put yourself in the buyers eyes and think how what would you want to see if you were buying this item. Think like that and supply those images. Remember the more images you have the better.

How to take a good photo

You will need a white background to take a basic photo for eBay. I suggest going to Wal-Mart or the dollar store and buy some poster board. I use the poster board to make my floor and background completely white. **Do not use flash on your camera**. Flash takes away from the items real look so turn the flash off and adjust the color and brightness using your computer image editing software. Every computer comes with some sort of software to be able edit color and brightness on an image. Even the basic photo viewer on a PC has color and brightness correction.

Duration

Some eBay experts suggest listing your items for seven days others say one day. I personally do not like the seven day listing only because most of the bidding takes place in the last two days. So I suggest either 3 or 5 day listings. You will be able to list more items and ultimately make more money faster than if you listed an item for 7 days.

The only items I would want on a seven day auction are antiques. Antiques with a seven day auction allow more people looking for that type of item to view and ultimately bid on those items.

Selling Manager

Selling manager is where you will go to track your items progress. From here you can see what sold and needs shipped, was is currently listed, if there are any bids on your listed items, how many watchers you have on a particular item, and if any items did not sell.

AFTER THE SALE

After the sale there is another important step to learn and get right. This is where you collect payment, print your shipping label, and get feedback.

Feedback

Feedback is crucial to your online success. People are wary of buying from a seller that even has only a few negative remarks. If you were to buy an item from someone, would you buy it from the guy with 100% positive feedback or 96% positive feedback? Properly stating your refund policy, providing exceptional communication and describing your item correctly are all important parts of doing business on eBay.

Give a packing slip

When you ship your item it will be to your benefit to include a packing slip. This will contain the item name, the cost to the buy as well as shipping costs. This is there receipt and most people do like to get one with their purchases.

Ask for positive feedback with your packing slip

When you print you packing slip also print on there somewhere a request for positive feedback if they are satisfied with their purchase. Also put something for your unhappy customers. Something like this "if you are unsatisfied with your purchase for any reason please contacts me immediately with the issue so we can resolve this as soon as possible."

How to pack items

Packing an item can be tricky for the first time seller, I personally use newspaper or bubble wrap when I ship my items. If you have something that is very fragile then you should pack it in a small box, and then pack that small box in a larger box. This will prevent damage in shipping. I always charge $0.50 for handling. This small charge will cover some of the material costs, as well as some of the fees that you will get for selling on eBay.

Buying postage online

I purchase all my postage online. This is faster and easier than waiting in line at the post office, plus you can just leave the package with the mail man and not have to even leave the house. To do this you will need either flat rate priority boxes, or regular boxes and a scale. I would suggest if you do not have a scale, to buy a small one, even a kitchen scale will work well. This is going to be the best idea for when you really start selling a lot of products.

If nothing else starts out with flat rate boxes then move into weighing your boxes. You will save your customers money and get more sales that way.

For larger boxes that go above what a normal kitchen scale can weigh I use my bathroom scale. Here is how

First I weigh myself.

Then I weight myself holding the package.

Take the two numbers and subtract them.

When you are finished you will be left with the package weight.

USPS ships packages based on one pound increments for priority mail. So you package that weighs 13 lbs. 8 oz. will cost the same as a package weighing 13 lbs. 15 oz.

This method of weighing is not idea but you need to enter a weight when you list your item.

You can also optionally take it to a post office and get it weighed there. For starting out I would sell small items that are easy to ship. The once you can get the hang of things you can move into larger items.

Collecting money through PayPal

PayPal is the best option to collect money from your buyers. This keeps the transactions legitimate and protected. You may also be able to accept credit cards and checks through PayPal. There is a $0.30 + 3% fee on all transactions processed through PayPal.

Rick Grubb

ADVANCED TECHNIQUES

Using these advanced techniques you will learn what products sell and how much they sold for.

What items sell best

The items that usually sell the best are

- Information Products such as how to guides, dvd's, books, and cd's

- Books

- software

- internet services

- anything on wheels

- collections

- children's clothing

- old, English china cups and saucers

- vintage jewelry

- media such as DVD's and CD's

- Dolls

- Dollar store items

- Anything your teens may like

- Musical Instruments

- Golf Clubs

- Name brand plus size clothing

- Purses, Shoes, and Boots

- Ski, snowboarding, and camping gear

- coins

- art

- props from movies

Research products to sell

In order to make educated guesses on what is

selling on eBay right now you need to know how to use eBay's search functions. First choose an item you would like to look up. Example: type in the search bar Hawaiian tropic shimmer effect.

Next click search. From there go over the end of the search bar and click advanced search.

On the advanced search screen you want to scroll down until you see the check box labeled completed listed.

Check this box and click search again.

Now you will be able to see what items were listed for that search term, if they did not sell the price will be red and if they did sell the price will be green. What I look for is a sell through rate of 28% or more which you can get by taking the first 20 or so items on the page and counting how many sold and dividing that number by however many there are. Also look for items with at least 50 items listed. Anything less than that and it may not be a good product to try to sell. Not right now anyways.

FINDING ITEMS IN THE STORE TO SELL ON EBAY

Using a notebook and pen method

When I am at store looking items to sell I do one of two things. I use the notebook method or the phone method. In the notebook method I write down the name of the product, the sale price, where I found it, and how many there were. Look for as many items as you can find. Next, go home and search eBay's completed listings and find ones that have that 28% sell through rate. If they are a good item they I will put an up arrow if they are not good I put a down arrow. Then next time I am out I will buy the items with the up arrow next to them.

This is a great way to find a lot of products fast. I use this method the most because it is easy and does not require cell phone access or an online connection. It allows me to find a lot of products fast and then research them all at once.

Using a smartphone to find items

Using a smartphone or a dumb phone with internet access is the next best thing to the notebook method. Just got m.ebay.com and search through the completed listings on your phone. The only reason why I don't like the method is because it is harder and takes up a lot of time to look up items vs. doing it at home and doing it on your desktop or laptop.

Finding niche products

Niche products are a good way to break into a market. If you just sold a bunch of one product research related products that you can buy that may sell equally as well. Example: helicopters sell really well. If a WL v911 sells well on eBay then I bet a similar model or brand will sell as well. Use this to capitalize on things that are already selling well.

WHERE ELSE TO FIND ITEMS TO SELL

EBay itself

EBay can be a good place to find items to sell. Look for listing that are not really well written of have no pictures. I bought a PDA for my online bookstore business on eBay for $37. The listing I bought it from had a weak description and no picture which kept buyers away. I could have easily turned around and sold that same product for $100+.

Target clearance

If you have ever walked into Target and paid attention, on the end caps of most of the isles are clearance or sale items. I have found some really great deals on clearance items at target. Just remember to take your notebook or phone with you and check the prices on some of these items. You can find a lot of winners shopping in the clearance sections of stores.

Dollar store

The dollar store that everything is actually only a dollar not Dollar General but Dollar Tree or The $.99 store is a good place to check. Do not expect to find much here though. These stores are loaded with a lot of stuff that's not worth even a dollar. I wanted to include it here because I have found some good stuff here though. The best way to really make out with purchases from here is selling them in a lot of in sets. I found some magic jacks here once and sold a lot of six of them for $20. I also found Criss Angel magic card decks where I bundles three decks together and sold them as a set for $9.99. So there is some money to be made just don't expect to become rich from it.

Libraries

Libraries are a good place to find books to sell. Almost all libraries have friends of the library book sales. You can get a list of libraries in your area at booksalefinder.com. In my book How To Start An Online Bookstore I cover how to find books to sell on Amazon or eBay exhaustively so please check it out for more information but there are a lot of shoppers on eBay and Half.com looking for a good book that you can pick up for pennies sometimes at these sales. I have noticed that How To books sells the best. Novels I do not bother with too much.

Bookstore bargain bins

Another good place to find books to sell is in the local bookstores bargain bins. Did I say local bookstore, what is that? Barnes and Noble is the largest bookstore right now so if you have one nearby you may be able to find some good deals. This is another place I would not hold my breath for finding good items to sell but it could happen.

Gabriel brothers

Gabriel Brothers is a clothing store that sells damaged or overstock clothes. I have found some really good deals here. The best deals are on hoodies. I have found sports team hoodies for other cities here for a fraction of what it would cost if they were nearby. Buy them and sell them on eBay for a nice profit.

Clothes

Clothes are the number one selling category on eBay. Do you shop at goodwill or have some of your own clothes you want to sell. Just be very descriptive when you list it. List how you wash it, cold water hot water, dryer, hang dry. You can really make living just selling clothes. Baby clothes are another hot item on eBay. If you have babies then you probably know what high selling clothes are and what are not. Just search goodwill or Salvation Army for some good deals.

Your own stuff

Selling your own stuff can be a great way to clean your house out and make some extra money. I start with small items that can ship easily. You would be surprised at how fast you can clean out the clutter when you sell some of your own stuff. This will be a good way to determine what sells and what does not as well. Once you sell some items you can then go look for them in stores later on.

Garage sales

Garage sales are a great place to find things to sell on eBay. People get rid of all kinds of things for a fraction of what they are worth. Going on the last day of the sale towards the end can also get you a good deal on all the stuff left over. Tell the owner if they would like they can sell you all the remaining items at a bulk price.

Family

Families are a good place to look when selling items on eBay. Offer to sell their stuff for them for a cut of the money. Usually you can take 25%-50% with no questions asked.

Attic

Clean out your attic. If you have not used to items in two years you probably do not need it right now. Sell it off on eBay and make some money while clearing out space at the same time.

Test with one product then sell multiple of the same just be relisting

If you found a product to sell while looking the places listed above test the market with one item then if you sell it you can just hit the re-list button. This is a great way to really streamline your listings. Just list it once and profit off of it for as many items as you can find. Remember it could take up to three times listed to sell an item. After three times it is safe to say the item is not a good seller and you should move on.

Where to store your inventory

It is best to designate a portion of your home to store your eBay inventory. You can use a shelf in the closet or even a space in your garage. It is good to have a place to put everything if you can to stay organized and keep everything together.

TRACKING SALES AND TAXES

Tracking sales

Use eBay's manage sales to track your current listing and sales.

Taxes

In the United States from my understanding you will only get tax forms if you have sold over 200 items plus $20,000 if you do not meet these requirements you will not be receive any tax forms from eBay for the year. EBay keeps records for you but just in case it is advised to save all your purchase receipts for a year or two.

CONCLUSION

EBay is a powerful selling site. Once you learn how to use it you will be hooked. Learning is the most difficult part of the process. Once you learn something you will know it forever. Take your time and learn the right way. There are tremendous supports forums on eBay that can help you get through any rough spots.

RESOURCES

How and where to locate the merchandise to sell on eBay or go to http://www.amazon.com/Where-Locate-Merchandise-Sell-ebook/dp/B002I65Y46

How to start an online bookstore or go to http://www.amazon.com/How-Start-Online-Bookstore-ebook/dp/B006FL9FZE

EBay for dummies or go to http://www.amazon.com/gp/product/1118098064

The Home Based Bookstore or go to http://www.amazon.com/gp/product/0977240606

How to buy sell and profit on eBay or go to http://www.amazon.com/gp/product/006076287X

Rick Grubb

HOW TO START AN ONLINE BOOKSTORE

Rick Grubb

How To Start an Online Bookstore Table Of Content

Why sell books online

Let me begin by saying, this is not a "get rich quick" scheme. Book selling is very easy to do but it will take some time to start. Do not let this discourage you. In my first month of selling books online I tripled my investment.

I will be laying out a great system; if you follow it, you will make money. This system, or style of book selling, is easy to start and easy to stick with. With as little as 30 minutes a week, you can start making some extra cash just like I did. So let's discuss some reasons why to get into book selling.

Online Book Sales Are Passing Up In-Store Book Sales

In today's world everyone shops online. Online book sales have actually surpassed book store sales. Why? There are larger selections of books at cheaper prices. It's easier and saves time.

Book Selling Online is Easy

Selling books online is as simple as entering a number or a title, clicking a button, setting a price, and submitting. I will be showing you exactly how to do all of this and more.

Book Selling Is Exciting

Imagine listing some books and waking up every day and having more orders to ship. Nothing is more exciting than accomplishing something you started for yourself. For me, it happened right away, and then I was hooked.

Now I have more than 100 books in my inventory, and it is still growing. Getting a steady supply of in-demand books is the key for your business to grow. I will go over every place you can look for books.

Good Turnover

Books that you select when following my advice will generally sell fast. For every batch of books I buy, I usually sell most, if not all, of them within four months of a book being listed. Books can be purchased cheaply from numerous different sources and sold for some pretty nice profits.

Easy To Ship

After your orders are rolling in, you will need to ship them. Books generally weigh less than 3 pounds, so shipping is low cost and easy to perform.

Profitable

You can do this full-time or sell books online part-time as a second income like I do.

Low Risk

If you follow my suggestions, book selling should be almost zero risk. You may buy some books that end up dropping below a reasonable selling price, but it's not that big of a deal as long as you follow my suggestions.

Low Start-Up Costs

For about $10, you can start today. When I started, I had nothing. Just $20 and a mindset that I wanted to make some extra money. Anyone can do this. You do not need special skills, a degree, or a lot of time. All you need to do is follow my advice and you will be on your way.

Getting Started as an Amazon Book Seller

Selling books online is easy. The site that I currently sell on, and recommend, is amazon.com. Amazon is the #1 online bookstore in the world. The user interface is easy to use, books sell for more money, and faster than any other site online. Amazon.com is the site that will be talked about throughout this book.

Sign Up For an Amazon Seller Account

Go to www.amazon.com and select "create a seller account." You will need a standard seller account in order to sell books on Amazon.

•The first step in signing up for an Amazon seller account is to click the "account" link on the homepage.

•Next, click "seller account".

•Enter your e-mail address and select "new customer".

•From there follow the instructions on setting up your account.

•You will need to set up a bank account so you can get paid. You should have this information ready ahead of time. What you need is your bank's routing number and your bank account number.

Other Important Steps

If you can afford to, use your Web service on your phone or purchase a personal data assistant from Amazon or eBay. I personally recommend a PDA or an Android Device. A PDA is what I use because I do not own a smart phone, or have a data package for my phone.

I purchased a PDA on eBay for $30, plus shipping. The only thing you need is a PDA with built-in Wi-Fi, and an SD or Compact Flash card slot. This will allow you, later in your business, to upgrade to a scanner tool if you choose. A PDA is an excellent choice for the beginner because it is able to be upgraded and used for many other things such as bookkeeping, e-mail, and listing items.

Where to Find Books

The outline in this book will show you how to buy a book for a dollar or less, and selling it for $10-$11, on average. In this chapter, I am going to tell you where I go for my most successful finds and hopefully where you can go as well.

Ongoing Library Sales

The most profitable place I find books to sell is at ongoing library sales. You can use the site www.booksalefinder.com to get the listings on which libraries have ongoing sales. These are usually small corner shelves or tables in the library, and are held daily during library hours.

This is the most successful place to find books to sell. With as little as 30 minutes of searching, I can walk away with $200-$300 worth of books.

Bookstore Bargain Bins

All Major bookstore chains have bargain bins which are usually located outside or right when you walk in the building. For the most part they are unloading a lot of junk. However, I have come across some really profitable books here. Usually there is more than one copy, so if you find a profitable book, buy all the copies you can find.

Library Sales

Library sales are held at almost every library at least once a year, but usually more often. The website booksalefinder.com is the best source to find upcoming library sales in your area. Just click your state, and it will show you all the sales for that month.

You can also click on your city, or nearby cities, for listing of when the next library sales will be. These can be very profitable, and most of them have preview sales. Make sure you go to preview sales early, as there are other people who go to the sales as well.

These sales are very cut throat. I personally avoid them, but I do know a lot of highly profitable books are sold there.

Goodwill and Salvation Army

Goodwill and Salvation Army are good places to look, but do not expect much from them. Call your local store to see which day of the week they have half-off sale on books. Most of them do, so you should go on those days. Again, go early, because other people will have the same idea.

Friends and Family

You may be related to one of your best sources. One of my big secrets to getting free books is getting them from friends and family. If they have any books they do not want, I offer to come over and remove them from their house for free. Most of them have so many books they do not want; they jump on the opportunity to have me come clear out the clutter.

Garage Sales

If you have a way to look up the prices or just feel like taking a gamble, almost everyone who holds a garage sale has books for sale. You can offer them a bulk price for the whole box of books, and then go home and look at what you got. This is kind of risky if you do not have a way to look up the prices, so do not pay too much for them.

As you continue with your business, you will find places to visit regularly. There are libraries I visit at least once a week, and there are others I will not even waste my time with anymore. You will learn as you go. As you do this more, you will know which books are new on the shelves and which ones you have seen already. This will make looking up books a much faster and easier process.

Finding books to sell

At this point you have learned what book selling has to offer, and where to start your search for books to buy. Next, I will go over the strategy that I use to find books to buy and sell.

A lot of books on the market that are about selling them go over how to pick books by guessing. This is a dangerous move, and can cost you money. For the best chance of success you will need either a web enabled cell phone or PDA. If you cannot afford a PDA there are other options as well.

Use the Library's Computer

If you cannot afford a web enables cell phone or PDA, there is a free technique to use. This is the most time-consuming but if it is the only option then it will do for now. Find a book to look up, and use the library's free computers to look up the price. Your best bet would be to find a batch of books to look up at the same time. Write down the ISBN numbers or the titles and look up the price on the computer. Once you begin to profit from your business, upgrade to a web-enabled cell phone or PDA.

Web-Enabled Cell Phone

Any phone that can access the internet will work. Almost every phone in use today is capable of accessing the Internet. Go to m.amazon.com and type in the book's ISBN number. This will bring up all the necessary information to make your buying decision.

Pocket PC, PDA with Wi-Fi

This is what I feel to be the most effective method. Why? With a PDA, you can use the library or bookstore's free Wi-Fi service. That means no expensive data package to access the Internet, fast page loads, and ultimately, more book look-ups. Also, with the PDA, once you really get rolling you can upgrade your PDA to a bar code scanner and get a subscription service such as Scout pal.

Smart Phones

If you have a smart phone, you can use it instead of a PDA. Also, Scout pal has a service available for smart phone users that allows them to take a picture of the bar code, and get the latest used price and sales rank data. If you do not have a smart phone, I strongly encourage you to buy a PDA.

Which books to sell

With the help of the library computer, cell phone, PDA, or smart phone you can look up prices before you pay for the book. Generally, when looking for books, I will not buy a book for more than a dollar. Also, I will not buy a book that will sell for fewer than five dollars. You are risking a loss by buying books that sell for under $5. At a selling price of $5 or more, you will still make a profit.

Sales Rank

Sales rank is used to determine how well a book is selling compared to every other book. In my system, you should not buy any book with a sales rank over 1 million. Amazon has currently over 8 million titles. A sales rank of 1 million will sell one book about once every other month. Unless the book is worth a lot of money try not to buy it if its sales rank is over 1 million.

Price Point

Price point is also very important. I came up with a chart that may help in the decision-making of buying books. Like I've said before, anything under $5 and you are risking a loss. To read this chart first check the sales rank of the book, and then check the lowest used price of the book. If both of those numbers match up according to the chart then I would suggest buying it.

Sales Rank - Used Selling Price

1-250,000 - $5

250,000-500,000 - $5 - $8

500,000-1,000,000 $8 - $10

1,000,000+ - $10 - $15

For example, if I pick up a book that is selling for $6.99, with a sales rank of 126,000, I would buy it. However, if that same book had a sales rank of 2,000,000, I would not buy it. Although this is just a guide, I have learned through experience that the higher the sales rank, the longer it will sit in your inventory. I also discovered the higher the sales rank, the less competition there is. The price point stays higher as well.

Amazon Fees

Amazon has higher fees than other book selling sites, but books will sell faster and for more money on Amazon. Amazon has a .99 cent fee for standard sellers, as well as a $1.35 fee per sale for everyone. Amazon also takes 15% of the total sale. Do not worry. If you buy a book for one dollar and sell it for $5 your profit will still be .90 cents. I know it doesn't sound like much, but it adds up. The majority of the time you will make a little extra money on shipping which helps pay for more books and supplies. The average amount I profit from a book is about $5, so all those books that I only make a few cents on help my bottom line.

How to List Books

In this chapter I will be going over how to list books on Amazon. We are going to go over looking up books, conditions, and shipping options

Looking Up Books

The first step is to look up the book you are going to sell. You may do this in two ways.

ISBN Number

The easiest way to look up a book is to type in the ISBN number. This is found on the back of the book near the bar code. If you do not have a dust jacket with the bar code or simply just do not see the ISBN numbers on the back of the book go to the copyright page. There you should find the ISBN number.

Title

Some books are older and do not have ISBN numbers. For these, you will need to look up the book by its title. Pay attention here, as there may be a paperback and hardcover version. People get really mad if you send them a hardcover and not a paperback book. Always, make sure you choose the right one.

Click Sell Yours Here

 On the books main page click sell your copy.

Put In the Condition of Your Book

The next step is to put in the condition of the book. Amazon has five conditions you can choose from. I always like to under evaluate my books. So if I list a book that looks to be "like new" I will call it very good. This will always get you better feedback because your buyer feels like he or she got more than expected.

New

The book is a brand-new and has never been read.

Like New

The book is still in perfect condition, but was not purchased as new.

Very Good

The book was read and shows very minimal signs of wear.

Good

The book was read, may have minimal highlighting, or writing, and may show some signs of wear.

Acceptable

The book shows major signs of wear. Corners or pages are bent, loose binding, highlighting marks, etc.

Condition Notes

Condition notes is where you want to add anything of importance. Things to be noted are:

Library Copy

Since most books are going to be from a library this will be your most used condition note.

Loose Binding

Any pages that are loose must be noted

Dust Cover, Missing or Damaged

If the book has a dust cover that is damaged or missing, you must tell your potential customers about it.

Highlighter or Any Other Markings

Does the book contain highlighting, or any markings?

Remainder Marks

A lot of clearance books from bookstores have a black line across the top or the bottom of the pages. Be sure to make reference to this in a condition notes.

After You Have Entered The Necessary Information Click "Continue".

Enter the Price You Wish To Sell It (Note: This Price Can Be Changed Later)

I always match the lowest price which can be found at the right side of the page.

Offer Multiple Shipping Options

It is always a good idea to offer standard shipping and expedited shipping. Once you have all the information filled in, click "submit listing".

Congratulations! You Have Successfully Listed Your First Book On Amazon.

Advanced Way to List Books

There is one other way to list books. This feature is new to Amazon but will be a much easier way to list books once you start using it.

- Log into your seller account

- Click view current inventory

- On the inventory screen there is a button called "Add a Listing"

- Once you click that you will then type in the ISPN number which will bring you to the screen were you will select the book to sell by clicking sell you're here

- The next screen is where you will enter condition, price, quantity, notes, shipping, and an option seller SKU.

- Finally click save and finish.

This is a more advanced way of listing but overall is easier once you do it a few times. I would suggest to those who are just starting out to learn both ways of listing books. Then decide for yourself which way is easier for you.

How to ship the books

Shipping is scary for some people. Now, however, with the assistance of online postage, you only need to click a few buttons.

Clean Up Books First

Clean up the book covers before you ship them. Peel off any stickers, clean off residue from the stickers, clean off any marks where you can, etc. Make your books look as nice as possible before you ship them. The easiest way of doing this is to use a solvent called Goo Gone. You can buy this almost anywhere.

Water-Seal the Books

In the case that the post office drops your book in a puddle of water, the book will still be intact if it is water sealed. There are two ways you can do this.

Plastic Bag

Place the book in the resalable plastic bag. Zip lock freezer bags work well. This is the best way to seal the book, but also the most costly.

Saran Wrap

Saran wrap is what I use. It is cheaper and I debate it being easier to use than a plastic bag. It also looks more professional.

Package the Book

Packaging the book is easy. I like to use 9 X 13 clasp envelopes. You can find them at Wal-Mart for about $3.49 for 25, and sometimes even the dollar store. You can also use packaging paper that looks like a roll of brown paper bag material.

Print Shipping Label

Now you will need to print your shipping label. You do this by clicking the "unshipped orders" button on your seller account main page. Next, weigh your book and put in the weight of your book where it says to enter the weight. Finally, you choose your carrier option, (i.e. media mail) and click print.

Daily tasks

Daily Tasks are the part of the business that no one wants to do. But to keep your business going strong you must do them. Daily tasks should be done on a scheduled basis. These tasks include price changes, bookkeeping, clearing old stock, etc.

Price Changes

The most important task I do daily, sometimes even twice a day, is price changes. To do this, log into your seller account, click manage current inventory. Here you will be able to see all the books in your inventory. I proceed to match any book that is not at the current lowest price, to the lowest price. Do not go lower that the current lowest price.

This happens online a lot, especially with books, and all it does is drive down the price. If you have a copy listed at the same price as someone else you will still get the sale depending on your location and condition. It is just throwing money away if you go under the current market price.

If a book falls below $3.00 I would remove it from my inventory because you can potentially lose money on the sale if it sells below that point. One easy way to match the prices on your inventory is to use the select all tab. Once you do that, click the action tab and select match lowest price. This will match all the books you selected to the lowest price. Just remember to remove or deselect any books that are under $3.00 first.

Bookkeeping

Bookkeeping is a very important task. Things you will need to record include purchases, shipping, net sales, and overall profit. The easiest way to do this is to keep a book and record the data for each month. Do not skip this step. The IRS will want records from Amazon if you make over $600 in the year. If you do not record any purchases you cannot write these purchases off. Always make sure you keep all of your receipts. You will only get taxed higher than you need to be.

Getting Rid of Old Stock

The time will come when space gets tight and books go below a profitable selling price. A good place to start is any book that the going price is under $3.00. At this point if your book is priced less than that you will lose money. It is better to donate the book and write it off on your taxes at the end of the year.

Advanced techniques

This chapter will teach you about optional advanced techniques that you can use. Techniques like using a barcode scanner, scouting service, and listing services. However I would not recommend this to anyone just starting out. Start slow and build up to this point.

Scout Pal

Scout Pal is a paid service that allows you to look up the price of books from your cell phone or PDA. This service allows you to get real time data on the current Amazon market price. That means current price of new and used books, as well as the Amazon sales rank.

You may also upload the current market data onto your PDA if you know you will be without Internet service. This technique is great if you are using a PDA and want to go to garage sales or thrift stores where Internet is not available. Scout Pal has a reasonable price at $9.95 a month.

A Seller Tool

Similar to Scout Pal is A Seller Tool. They offer phone scanning where you manually enter prices onto your phone. You may also get the PDA package where you can enter prices onto a PDA or scan them with a barcode scanner. The phone scanning will run you $6.99 a month, and the PDA scanning will run you $29.99 a month.

Out of the two services I would lean more towards Scout Pal. They both offer good services but Scout Pal seems to have more options at a better price. You may try both for free, as both have a free trial.

Barcode Scanners

With the use of a barcode scanner and a scouting service you can scan books quickly and cover a lot more ground than if you were manually typing ISBN numbers in.

These scanners come in handy mainly for large book sales where people line up in the morning before the sale to get first pick at it. With a scanner you can find books more efficiently than the other people and pick your books before they can even look at it.

I would definitely recommend not spending the money on a scanner or a scouting service until you get some experience and are sure this is something you want to do. Remember the scouting services do have a monthly fee involved so you want to have a steady supply of books to get every month. Advanced techniques like this are defiantly something to consider down the road in your business.

Amazon Pro Merchant

Becoming an Amazon Pro Merchant will be another great step, once you have a great system rolling. This technique will help greatly boost your sales. By becoming a pro merchant you wave the .99 listing fee Amazon charges you when you sell a book. Also you can have access to more seller tools and can utilize even more programs to help you get your inventory online. The cost of this service is $39.99 per month.

Book Listing Programs

Book listing programs are special programs that help you manage your inventory over multiple selling sites such as eBay, half, and Abe books. With the use of these programs you can edit pricing and handle more business without having to log into every site. Here are some of the top programs to use

Fillz.com

bookrouter.com

theartofbooks.com

Remember you do not need to use any of these techniques outlined in this chapter, they are simply for someone who is looking to do this full time and wants assistance where they can get it.

Putting it all Together

Throughout this book you have learned everything from setting up an account to listing your first books. To go over everything we have done let's just review.

Chapter 1 we learned why you should get into book selling.

Chapter 2 we learned about selling books on Amazon.com and setting up our account.

Chapter 3 we learned where the best places to find books are and my favorite place which is ongoing library sales.

Chapter 4 we learned about looking up books and different devices you may use to look them up with.

Chapter 5 we learned which books to buy, which books to pass on, sales rank, buying signals, and Amazon fees.

Chapter 6 we learned how to list books, what the different conditions are, and what the different notes to include in the condition notes.

Chapter 7 we learned how to clean, water seal, package, and ship books

Chapter 8 we learned how about price changes, bookkeeping, and clearing old stock.

Chapter 9 we learned about scouting programs and book listing programs

I want to take this time to congratulate you. If you follow my system as outlined you have a really good chance of making money. I do everything I outlined here and have made a great extra income. As with everything, the more work you put into it, the more money you can potentially make. Just believe in yourself and you will succeed.

About The Author

Thank you for purchasing my book. I started learning how to make money online when I was about 19 years old. Since, I have learned a number of techniques that anyone can use to bring a good second income using the Internet.

During the day I am a full time pastry chef. I have a two year degree in baking and pastry arts from Pennsylvania Culinary Institute. All of my online adventures have been self-taught. It has been a long but fun journey for me, and I am proof that you can do whatever you put your mind to.

I say this because I really struggled with English since I was a little kid, and now I am a freelance writer for Yahoo.com, my own website, and an author of many books.

I also would like to say thank you to my wife Sheryl. Without her I would have had a much more difficult time putting this book that you just read together. Thank you again for your support, I hope you enjoy the book.

Warning and Disclaimer:

This book is for your personal enjoyment only. You may not sell or give away any content in this book. This book describes the authors own results selling books online. Results found in this book are not guaranteed. This book does not offer any legal or financial advice.

Every effort has been taken to ensure that all the material in this book is correct. However, this book still may contain errors, or outdated information. The author is not responsible for any losses that may occur from the use or alleged use of this book.

This book is a guide and additional sources may need to be consulted in addition to this book. Sources and further readings are located throughout this book.

Rick Grubb

Individual results may vary

Resources

Books

- The Home Based Bookstore
- The $100 Startup

My Other Books for Sale You May Like

- The Lean Startup Guide: How to Take an Idea to Success with Little to No Money
- How to Write and Sell Articles on the Kindle, Nook, iPad, and Other E-readers

Review Request

Reviews are important to the success of a book. If you enjoyed this book please go to the sales page on Amazon and leave a positive review. You may do so by visiting

http://www.amazon.com/Sell-Used-Items-Amazon-ebook/dp/B00BSIFCLK

and click on write a customer review in the customer reviews section of the page.

If for any reason you did not like this book please contact me directly at ricgrb1@gmail.com and let me know why you did not like it so that I can update it to better suit your expectations.